CRAFT BOX

TUDOR TIMES

12 projects to make and do

Published in 2015 by Wayland
Copyright © Wayland 2015

Wayland
338 Euston Road
London NW1 3BH

Wayland Australia
Level 17/207 Kent Street
Sydney, NSW 2000

Editor: Elizabeth Brent
Designer: Rocket Design (East Anglia) Ltd
Craft stylist: Annalees Lim
Photographer: Simon Pask, N1 Studios

The website addresses (URLs) listed in this book are correct at
the time of going to press. However, it is possible that contents
or addresses may have changed since the publication of this book.
No responsibility for any such changes can be accepted by either
the author or the Publisher.

Picture acknowledgements:
All step-by-step craft photography: Simon Pask, N1 Studios; images
used throughout for creative graphics: Shutterstock with the
exception of p5, tr iStock photo.

A cataloguing record for this title is available at the British Library.
Dewey number: 942'.05-dc23

First published in 2013 by Wayland

ISBN: 978 0 7502 8405 9

10 9 8 7 6 5 4 3 2

Printed in China

Wayland is a division of Hachette Children's Books, an
Hachette UK company.

Contents

the Tudors

The Tudor family ruled England and Wales for more than 100 years. Tudor kings and queens, such as King Henry VIII and Queen Elizabeth I, are some of the most famous monarchs in British history.

The Tudor monarchs reigned from 1485–1603 CE

In Tudor times, cities and towns grew as houses, shops, schools and theatres were built for a growing population. The wealthy paid artists to paint their portraits, and writers, including William Shakespeare, to write plays for theatres. Tudor ships sailed around the world, exploring new lands and bringing back spices, silks and plants such as potatoes and tobacco. New navigation tools and skills helped explorers to map newly discovered lands like America.

Tudor craftsmen were skilled at working with materials including wood, metals, gems and leather. Each group of craftsmen were members of a guild, like modern trade unions.

Some craftsmen worked as travelling journeymen, others in workshops. Big houses, colleges and churches often had their own workshops with apprentices and journeymen working under a master craftsman.

The buildings and objects they made can tell us a lot about the way people lived in Tudor times: the clothes they wore, how they decorated their homes and the games they played. They can also inspire you to make some Tudor crafts of your own!

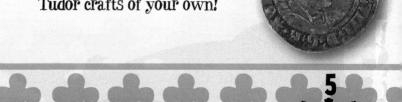

make a
Tudor rose

The Tudor rose is a symbol of the union between two families, the Lancasters and the Yorks. When King Henry VII married Elizabeth of York, the white rose of York and the red rose of Lancaster were joined to represent the new royal family: the Tudors.

1 Draw a star with five points, measuring about 6 or 7cm across, onto a piece of green felt and cut it out.

2 Cut out a piece of red felt in the shape of a flower with five petals. Glue it on top of the green felt, so that the five green points are just showing.

3 Cut a smaller flower shape with five petals from white felt and glue this in the middle of the red flower.

Cut a circle of yellow or gold felt big enough to fill the centre of the white flower. Glue the yellow circle onto the middle of the white rose.

5

If you are using an old badge, glue the badge and press the green felt onto it. If you are using a safety pin, use a needle and thread to sew it to the green felt.

Did you know...
Tudor roses appear on the UK's royal coat of arms.

7

make a
Masquerade mask

Masquerade balls were popular in Tudor times. Guests wore masks to hide their identity. The fashion for wearing masks came from medieval entertainers called mummers, and from Italian mask carnivals.

1 Draw a mask shape onto the card and cut it out. Mark the eyeholes and cut them out.

2 Use the pencil and ruler to mark out areas you want to paint in different colours, and then go over these lines using the marker pen. Colour some of the sections in black.

3 Paint the remaining sections using acrylic paints.

4 Paint the craft stick using acrylic paints and glue or tape it to the back of the mask.

5 Glue or tape feathers to the top of the mask, and curly ribbon to the sides of the mask.

6 Use glitter glue or sequins to decorate your mask.

Did you know...
Masks were worn by players in musical entertainments called masques and mummeries.

make a Jester's crown

Jesters were popular entertainers on the streets and at the Royal Court in Tudor times, playing the fool, singing funny songs and telling jokes. They wore colourful costumes and hats like floppy crowns, decorated with bells.

1 Cut a strip of craft foam 5cm wide and long enough to fit around your head plus 3cm. Staple the ends together to form a band.

2 Use the template to cut ten triangles of craft foam in different colours. Cut five of the triangles in half, and then glue one half-triangle to the front of each whole triangle and one to the back on the opposite side. Leave to dry.

3 Glue or staple the triangles to the band, lining up the base of each triangle with the bottom of the band. Space the triangles to cover the band.

4

Glue a craft bell to the pointed end of each triangle or sew it on using a needle and thread.

5

Decorate the band by gluing on fake gems or sequins or triangles, circles and squares cut from different-coloured craft foam.

Did you know...
Tudor street entertainers included acrobats, jugglers and tightrope walkers.

make a
Jester's stick

Jesters' costumes made them look like comical kings. They carried sticks shaped like royal sceptres, with bells to shake as they told jokes or did pranks to amuse and entertain the Royal Court.

You will need:
+ Dowel or craft stick
+ Styrofoam ball about 8cm in diameter
+ Glue
+ Acrylic paints
+ Brushes
+ Craft foam or construction paper
+ Pair of compasses and pencil
+ Scissors
+ Coloured ribbons
+ Small craft bells

1 Push one end of the stick into the Styrofoam ball and glue in place.

2 Paint the ball and craft stick or dowel using acrylic paints. Allow them to dry.

3 Draw two concentric circles, measuring 4cm and 12cm in diameter, on foam or construction paper and cut them out.

4

Cut away the outer circle to make a flower shape. Cut out the inner circle and push the collar onto the stick under the ball.

5

Cut six pieces of ribbon of different lengths up to 12cm long. Thread a craft bell onto the end of each and tie a knot to hold it on. Tie the other end of the ribbon under the collar on the stick. Cover the knots with another piece of ribbon.

6

Decorate the Styrofoam ball by gluing on more ribbon and craft foam, and wind ribbon around the craft stick.

Did you know...
Favourite jesters were housed, clothed and fed in the Tudor Royal Court.

make a
Tussie mussie

The Tudors used scented flowers and herbs to hide bad smells and keep away 'bad air', which they thought carried diseases such as the plague. They pinned small, scented posies, called tussie mussies or nosegays, to their clothes.

1 Cut the flower stem and sprigs to the same length. Gather them into a tight bunch with the flower at the centre and secure with tape or a rubber band.

2 Cut a small piece of foil and wrap it tightly around the ends of the sprigs.

3 Cut a small hole in the centre of the coaster or doily. Push the foil end of the posy through the hole.

4

Gather the doily around the posy to form a collar and tape it in place.

5

Decorate the tussie mussie with trails of curly ribbon or raffia.

Did you know...

Tussie may come from a word meaning a knot of flowers, and mussie from the damp moss that was wrapped around them to keep them moist.

make a
model of a
Tudor house

Tudor houses were built on timber frames with panels of 'wattle and daub', made by smearing straw, mud or animal dung onto twigs and branches. Black tar on the beams and whitewashed panels created the 'half-timbered', or black and white, style.

1 Turn a box on its side and glue or tape it to another box to create an overhanging gallery floor.

2 Cut and fold the third box to make a roof. Tape it in place on top of the boxes.

3 Mix a little sand into white acrylic paint and brush it onto the sides of the house. Allow it to dry.

4

Cut strips of black paper and glue them onto the sides of the building to form the beams. Look at pictures of Tudor houses in books and on the Internet to give you ideas.

5

Draw a door and some windows onto the card, cut them out and stick them to the front of the building.

6

Glue matchsticks, straw or short pieces of raffia onto the roof in overlapping rows to make a thatched roof.

Did you know...

Tudor houses were built with overhanging galleries to add space on higher storeys and avoid paying ground rent tax.

make a
Tudor ruff

Wealthy people in Tudor times wore frilled collars called ruffs, made from fine linen and lace. The ruffs could be washed separately from their clothes, and were starched and pressed by special 'goffering' irons.

You will need:
+ Five round paper doilies
+ Scissors
+ Three sheets of white paper
+ Glue
+ Hole punch
+ Ribbon
+ Large needle

1

Fold the doilies into quarters and cut off the points.

2 Fold each sheet of paper widthways to make a clear fold and then open it out again. Glue the doily edges along both long sides of each sheet of paper and allow to dry.

3 Make concertina folds backwards and forwards along each sheet of white paper, making each fold about 2cm wide. Hold the pleats together and cut each sheet in half using the fold line as a guide.

4

Hold the pleats together and punch a hole about 2cm in from the edge of each section.

5

Glue the folded sheets together along the short edges to make a ruff long enough to fit around your neck, with 3cm to spare.

6

Use the needle to thread the ribbon through the hole, then draw the ruff pleats together.

Did you know...

Some ruffs measured 30cm across and needed wire frames to support them.

make a
Stained glass coat of arms

In Tudor times, heraldic badges or coats of arms showed who your family was or where you came from. Families displayed coats of arms on clothes, armour, shields and flags, and on the walls and windows of their houses.

1 Fold a piece of black paper in half, and cut a half-shield shape along the fold line.

2 Keeping the shield shape folded in half, cut away a rectangle and a quarter circle, leaving a horizontal strip in the middle.

3 Open the shield shape up. Cut a strip of black paper and glue it onto the back down the middle to form four sections.

4

Cut a piece of blue cellophane and glue or tape it onto the back of two diagonally opposite sections. Repeat using red cellophane to complete the shield.

5

Cut two fleur-de-lys shapes and two Tudor roses from the gold paper. Glue one onto each section of the shield.

Did you know...
Rich Tudors sometimes had their family portraits painted onto glass window panes.

make a
Tudor cap

Hats were worn by people of all ages in Tudor times. The poor wore simple woollen caps, but rich men wore caps made from silk, velvet or wool, often decorated with jewelled bands and feathers.

You will need:
+ Pencil or pen
+ Two sheets of craft foam
+ Scissors
+ Fabric
+ Stapler
+ Fabric glue
+ Fake gems
+ Two feathers

1 Draw two concentric circles on the craft foam, one measuring 30cm across and the other 12cm across. Cut out the circles, to make two rings of craft foam.

2 Cut out two circles of fabric measuring 12cm wider than the foam rings. Staple one of the fabric circles to one of the foam rings to form the 'crown' of the cap.

3 Snip around the edges of the other fabric circle. Cut out the centre, and glue it to the second foam ring to form the 'brim' of the cap.

4

Glue the crown of the cap to the brim.

5

Stick some gems to a piece of craft foam and cut out the shape to make a decorative badge.

6

Decorate the cap by gluing the feathers and the badge to the front.

Did you know...

A law in 1571 made all men and boys over six wear a woollen cap on a Sunday to help the wool trade!

make a Ship's figurehead

In Tudor times, many ships had carved wooden figureheads. Traditionally, they were seen as the ship's eyes, lending it protection and helping anyone who could not read to identify the ship.

You will need:

+ Plastic spray bottle
+ Funnel
+ Sand
+ Aluminium foil
+ White glue and water
+ Tissue paper
+ String
+ Cardboard
+ Scissors
+ Acrylic and metallic paints
+ Brushes
+ Card
+ Red felt pen
+ Stapler

1 Remove the spray cap and make sure the bottle is clean and dry. Using the funnel, pour a little sand inside to add weight, then replace the cap.

2 Using the foil, mould the shape of a lion onto the bottle. Use long 'sausages' to mould the legs and mane, and small balls to build up the shape of the face. Secure in place with more foil.

3 Make papier maché by tearing tissue paper into strips and dipping them into a mix of equal parts white glue and water. Cover the figure in papier maché and leave it to dry.

4

Cut some short pieces of string and glue them in swirling shapes onto the papier maché to form the mane and fur. Cut a shield from cardboard and glue it to the front of the figure.

5

Paint your figurehead using acrylic paints. Use metallic paint to go around the shield and for the fur and claws. When it is dry, use black acrylic paint to paint the face.

6

Use the card to make a crown and the decoration for the shield, and then stick them to the figure.

Did you know...
The figurehead of the famous Tudor ship 'the Mary Rose', was a Tudor rose.

make a
Cup and ball

Tudor children played with simple toys, often carved from wood. The cup and ball was a popular game of catch. Children swung the ball on a string into the air and tried to catch it in the cup.

1 Tape the bottom of the cup to one end of the cardboard tube.

2 Using the skewer or knitting needle, make a hole through the centre of the Styrofoam ball.

3 Paint the cone and the ball two contrasting colours.

4 Decorate the cone, using masking or electrical tape to make stripes.

5 Cut a length of wool or string about 20cm long and thread the needle. Push the needle through the hole in the Styrofoam ball and make a knot in the end of the string to hold it to the ball.

6 Make a hole in the cup and thread the other end of the string through it. Make a large knot inside to hold it firmly in place.

Did you know...
Other wooden toys included hoops, spinning tops, skittles and rattles.

make a Tudor peg doll

Dolls in Tudor times were often made from scraps of fabric, odds and ends or clothes pegs. Some were homemade, others were sold by travelling salesmen called pedlars.

You will need:
+ Scraps of fabric/lace
+ Scissors
+ Wooden clothes peg
+ Glue
+ Ribbon
+ Pipe cleaner
+ Felt pens
+ Wool
+ White paper
+ Ruler
+ Gold braid

1 Cut a circle of fabric, making the radius the same size as the height of the peg. Cut a small hole in the centre.

2 Push the peg through the hole and glue the fabric onto it, leaving the top of the peg showing. Tie a piece of ribbon around the middle of the peg to secure the fabric and make a waist.

3 Cut a pipe cleaner in half and glue it onto the peg to make arms. Twist the ends to make small hands.

Draw a face onto the peg. Cut short pieces of wool and glue them on to make hair.

Cut a semi-circle from some colourful fabric to make a cape or a jacket. Glue under the arms to hold it in place.

6

Make a ruff by concertina-ing a strip of white paper and gluing it to the doll's neck. Cut a piece of gold braid and glue it to the wool to form a hair band.

Did you know...
In Tudor times, dolls were known as 'wooden babies'.

Glossary

Apprentice A young person learning a skilled trade or craft.

Beam A length of wood, metal or stone that supports a building or roof.

Carnival A type of festival or fair.

Dung Toilet waste from animals.

Figurehead A carved wooden figure fixed to the front of a ship.

Fleur-de-lys A three-petal representation of a lily.

Goffering iron An iron that is used to press folds or pleats.

Guild A group formed by people with the same job or skills.

Heraldic To do with the coats of arms of noble families.

Journeyman An assistant craftsman, sometimes hired by the day.

Linen A fabric made from a plant called flax.

Masquerade A dance at which guests wear masks and costumes.

Medieval From the Middle Ages, the period of history which lasted from about 1000–1500 CE.

Monarch A king or queen.

Navigation The art of finding your way at sea or on land.

Plague A deadly disease in Tudor times.

Portrait A painting of a person.

Posy A small bunch of flowers.

Reign The period of time that a king or queen rules for.

Royal Court The household that is centred on the king or queen.

Sceptre A ceremonial staff carried by a monarch.

Tar A black, sticky substance mostly made from coal.

Timber Wood prepared for building.

Whitewash A mixture of lime and water, used to paint walls white.

Further information

BOOKS

Explore: Tudors by Jane Bingham (Wayland, 2014)

The Gruesome Truth About the Tudors by Jillian Powell (Wayland, 2010)

Hail! Tudors by Philip Steele (Wayland, 2013)

History Relived: The Tudors by Cath Senker (Wayland, 2009)

Horrible Histories: The Terrible Tudors by Terry Deary (Scholastic, 2007)

Men, Women and Children in Tudor Times by Jane Bingham (Wayland, 2011)

WEBSITES

http://www.bbc.co.uk/schools/primaryhistory/famouspeople/henry_viii/
Visit this BBC website for lots of information about the Tudor King Henry VIII.

http://www.hrp.org.uk/PalaceKids/discover/allabouttudors
Snappy facts about the Tudor period, plus a family tree tracing the British monarchy back to the Tudors.

http://horrible-histories.co.uk/
The Horrible Histories website has some fun Tudor games and jokes.

http://resources.woodlands-junior.kent.sch.uk/homework/tudors/timeline.htm
A detailed interactive timeline of the Tudor period.

Index